DRUGS

Adrian King

WAYLAND

Editor: Carron Brown
Consultant: Ruth Hilton
Designer: Rita Storey, StoreyBooks
Cover Designer: Giles Wheeler, Dome Design
Production controller: Carol Titchener

First published in 1997 by Wayland Publishers Ltd, 61 Western Road, Hove,

East Sussex, BN3 1JD. Find Wayland on the internet at http://www.wayland.co.uk

The publishers would like to thank the staff and pupils of Uplands Special School in

Brighton for their advice and support.

British Library Cataloguing in Publication Data

King, Adrian 1946-

Drugs. – (Face the Facts)

    1. Drugs – Juvenile literature 2. Drug abuse – Juvenile literature

    I. Title

    362.2'9

ISBN 0 7502 1756 1

Typeset by StoreyBooks, England

Printed and bound by G Canale in Turin, Italy

Picture acknowlegements

Danny Allmark cover; Eye Ubiquitous/J. Burke 33, /Roger Chester 7, /Patrick Field 15 (bottom), /Paul Seheult

11 (top), 15 (top), 24 /Skjold 6 (bottom); Sally and Richard Greenhill/Sam Greenhill 9 (top); David Hoffman

11 (bottom), 16, 22, 28, 30, 31, 36 (bottom); Impact Photos/Peter Arkell 35 (top), /Vera Lentz 31, /Simon Shepheard

32; Pictor International 14 (bottom), 34, 43; Popperfoto 39; Reflections Photo Library/Rex Moreton 10,

/Jenny Woodcock 6 (top), 8, 12, 14 (top), 38, 42; Science Photo Library/Oscar Burriel 40, /Vaughan Fleming 26,

/John Heseltine 41, /Saturn Stills 36 (top), /Sinclair Stammers 37; Topham Picturepoint 9 (bottom); Wayland

Picture Library 20, /Tizzie Knowles 35 (bottom); Zefa 13.

The illustrations on pages 8, 15, 17, 19, 21, 23, 25 and 28 are

by Rachel Fuller.

Photo shoots directed by Bridget Tily.

Most of the people who appear in this book are models.

Thank you to the models and their agent Grace Jackman.

CONTENTS

ABOUT DRUGS

SOME drugs are medicines that help you to get well if you are ill. Some drugs do not help you to get well. Instead, they may hurt you or make you feel bad if you do not know what they are, or what they are used for.

This book is here to help you understand
- some of the drugs you might see in your house, at school, in hospitals, in doctors' clinics or on sale in shops, pubs or on the street
- the ways that some people may use drugs
- the reasons why people use drugs
- the law and what it says about drugs
- how drugs can be harmful

This book will help you understand more about drugs. It does not try to tell you what you should do, but it may help you decide. If you are ever unsure what to do, you can always ask someone you trust to help you. It must be someone sensible, who knows about drugs and who knows you well, too. You always need to be able to take care of yourself, or to know someone else who can take care of you.

The word 'drug' is used to mean different things. It can mean 'medicine', 'legal drug' or 'illegal drug'.

`Medicines` are used to help sick people get well. Many medicines can only be given to you if the doctor says so. These are called prescription medicines.

`Legal drugs` are drugs that the law allows you to take. Some drugs, such as alcohol and nicotine, cannot be sold to you until you reach a certain age.

`Illegal drugs` are drugs that the law does not let you have. It is a crime to have any of these drugs.

This book will describe all three kinds. All drugs can change the way you think, feel or act.

ALL ABOUT YOU

Before looking at drugs, think about yourself and what makes you important. What makes you special? What makes you different from other people? What do you like to do or to eat? What makes you laugh? What are you good at? What do you want to do when you are older? Think about all these things – no one else is quite the same as you. The way you look, speak, think and behave make you different from everyone else. What makes you laugh and cry? What do your friends like about you and what don't they like? Are there things you don't like about yourself? You cannot change your height or the way you look, but there are things about you that you can change. Everyone can get better at things they do.

Frank: 'I am friendly and don't get upset easily. I can run pretty well too. Chinese take-aways and *Eastenders* are cool. I don't like football much and I'm not much good at maths or art. I would like to be better looking. I would love to own my own shop one day.'

Donna: 'I am a bit moody. I like Boyzone and I enjoy acting. I find it hard to make friends. We end up having rows. I want to learn not to get angry so easily.'

Staying healthy

When you are ill you may feel very unhappy. Your health is important. Health is about being well and feeling good. Drugs can sometimes help you to get well. Your doctor can tell you which ones may help.

Sometimes, even when you are well you can feel unhappy. Maybe things are going badly, or you have argued with someone. It is good to have someone to talk to, or special things to think of, such as the future.

Healthy bodies only stay well if you treat them with care.
- **Eat fruit and vegetables.**
- **Have a balanced diet.**
- **Get plenty of sleep (at least eight hours a night).**
- **Only take medicines when doctors advise it.**
- **Keep yourself safe.**
- **Get plenty of fresh air and exercise.**

▲ Some dreams may never come true for you, such as winning the lottery or being an Olympic champion, but everyone can look forward to improving their skills and doing things well.

Your friendships and your feelings

Friends can make all the difference to how you feel. If friends are unkind, it can feel like the end of the world. Choose your friends carefully.

The best friends are people who like you for who you are, and who respect your views. Do you argue with other people if they have different ideas from yours, or do you let them say what they feel?
Friends should trust each other. A friend you can trust may be the person you turn to when things go wrong. That is when friendship matters most.

▼ If friends are kind to you, it feels great.

> 66 **Mark:** 'I like a challenge. I often go on weekends away organized by the youth club. We climb rock faces using strong ropes. Without them, I would not be safe. I always try to be careful. Otherwise, I might get hurt.' 99

Taking risks

How do you spend your free time? Perhaps you ride a bike, swim, listen to music or watch television. Sometimes, it's good to hang around with friends and not do much, either at someone's house or out in town.

What might happen when there is a risk of danger? If you take a risk and get away with it, that's lucky. Is risk-taking sensible or stupid? Can it be both? Are some risks impossible to avoid? Only you can decide whether a risk is too big to take. You are special, so decide with care! You need to know what you are doing. You deserve to stay safe – from drugs or any other kind of danger.

> 66 **Janine:** 'I get to my friend's house by bike. I don't have any lights for my bike even though it is getting dark when I go home. I don't own a bike helmet, either. I know I might be taking risks but the road I cycle on is very quiet.' 99

9

DIFFERENT DRUGS
DRUGS AND MEDICINES

WHEN you are ill, you may need medicine to help you get well. Medicines are drugs. Your doctor may tell you what you need or, if you have something mild like a headache, you might use a drug such as paracetamol, sold by chemists. Medicines always have instructions on the packet or bottle. If the doctor has chosen the drug, it will have your name on the bottle and special instructions just for you.

Not all drugs are medicines

Beer and wine contain a drug called alcohol. Tea and coffee contain a drug called caffeine. Cigarettes contain another drug called nicotine. The people who take these are not usually ill, they just take them. There are other drugs that are not medicines too, such as Ecstasy (*see* page 16), amphetamine (*see* page 22), LSD *(see* page 28) and cannabis (*see* page 26).

This girl is taking a medicine called paracetamol to help her clear her headache. It is important to read the instructions before taking any ◀ medicine.

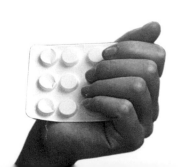

There are four main groups of drugs
- medicines
- drugs people take openly
- **legal drugs people often hide**
- illegal drugs

`Legal` `drugs` means there is no law to stop you. `Illegal` `drugs` means the law does not let you take them. Parents and schools have rules about drugs even if they are legal ones.

▲ These products are legal, but did you know that they all contain drugs.

You need to find out what these rules are. Legal does not mean the same as safe. Sometimes, legal drugs can be very harmful.

Why do people take drugs?

People who take drugs that are not medicines often take them because they like the way these drugs make them feel. Sometimes, they want to know what it feels like to try them. Usually, these drugs have no instructions. This means it is harder to know whether you will stay safe. Some people choose not to take drugs even when they are ill. There are people who choose to take some drugs but not others. Some find it hard to stop once they have become used to a drug they have tried.

This teenager thinks she looks cool. ▶
What do you think?

STIMULANTS, HALLUCINOGENS, DEPRESSANTS AND PAINKILLERS

Medicines are very carefully made and they are pure. There are instructions on the bottle or packet.
But with other drugs you can never be sure what the effects will be on someone who takes them.

People who take amphetamine too often can become very frightened.

If you expect to feel miserable when you drink alcohol, you probably will!

What determines the kind of effect a drug can have on you?

- The amount you take (called the dose)
- How often you take the drug (called the frequency)
- How you feel when you take the drug (called your mood)
- What you think will happen (called your expectation)
- What is in the drug (called its purity)
- How your body reacts to the drug

Lisa: 'One night I think I drank too much alcohol. I felt very sick and fell over a lot. I can't remember much of what I said or did, and I felt really terrible in the morning.'

Addictive drugs

With some drugs, after a person has got used to taking them, his or her body starts to need the drug in order to work properly. After that, the body starts to feel bad if it doesn't have any.

If you take an 'E' that has a lot of MDMA in it, the effect will be strong. If there is not much MDMA but caffeine instead, the effect may be more like drinking several cups of coffee!

Drugs that act this way are called addictive drugs. The bad feelings people get when they need a drug and don't have it are called withdrawal symptoms. With some addictive drugs, such as alcohol or sleeping tablets, withdrawal symptoms can be very bad indeed. Many drugs can be overdosed on. An overdose means taking such a large dose that the bad effects of a drug become serious.

The four most common groups of drugs are
- stimulants
- hallucinogens
- depressants
- painkillers

Drugs might be swallowed, smoked, sniffed or injected. Injecting drugs leaves ugly puncture marks on the skin and can be deadly if dirty needles are used.

STIMULANTS, HALLUCINOGENS

Stimulants

Stimulants are drugs that make you feel wide awake, but not hungry. They are called stimulants because they stimulate the body's nervous system, making it more active. They can make you feel like you have a lot of energy. Later, you will probably feel really tired and hungry.

Coffee contains caffeine.

These drugs are stimulants

- caffeine (in tea, coffee and cola drinks)
- nicotine (in cigarettes and cigars)
- 'poppers' (their real names are amyl nitrite and butyl nitrite)
- cocaine and crack (different forms of the same drug)
- Ecstasy (can look like tablets or capsules)
- anabolic steroids (sometimes taken by athletes who think it will make their muscles stronger)
- amphetamine (tablets or powder – sometimes called 'speed')

Hallucinogens

Hallucinogens are drugs that make the world seem a different, strange place. You may see things that are not there. Sometimes these things do not seem to be friendly.

These drugs are hallucinogens

- LSD or 'acid' (often the drug is soaked into paper squares)
- magic mushrooms (they are real mushrooms that grow in the wild)
- Ecstasy (a hallucinogen as well as a stimulant)
- cannabis (*see* picture on the right) (may be dried leaves or a hard block of resin)

Depressants

Depressants are drugs that slow the body down and can make you relax and feel sleepy. They make it hard to concentrate, or keep your balance! Taking too much of a depressant drug can be very dangerous indeed.

These drugs are depressants

- alcohol (in beer, wines, spirits and alcoholic lemonades)
- tranquillizers (doctors may give them to people feeling anxious or depressed)
- sleeping tablets
- glue (some types are used as drugs)
- lighter fuel (usually a gas called butane)

▲ There are many alcoholic lemonades available. You have to be eighteen or older to be able to drink them legally.

Painkillers

Painkillers are drugs that help take pain away. Headache tablets are painkillers. They can make also you feel sleepy, and taking too many at one time can even make you unconscious or kill you.

These drugs are painkillers

- paracetamol (tablets or capsules – Lem-sip and Calpol contains paracetamol)
- heroin (a strong drug made from opium poppies)
- codeine (sometimes used for stomach upsets)
- morphine (used in hospitals when someone is badly hurt)

◄ Heroin is made from the sap of opium poppies.

15

ECSTASY

Ecstasy is a hallucinogen and a stimulant. This drug is illegal. It can also be called 'E', or names such as Love Doves, Dennis the Menace or Disco Biscuit. Its proper name is MDMA which stands for MethyleneDioxyMethAmphetamine.

Ecstasy may also be available as ▶ pills or coloured capsules.

Why do people take Ecstasy?

- Ecstasy makes you feel wide awake.

- Even if you dance a lot you won't feel tired.

- You will not feel hungry.

- What you see, feel and hear will be different.

- Music sounds very strange.

- The effects last a long time.

The risks and bad points

- It starts by making you feel a bit sick.

- It can make your jaw stiff and your heart beats faster.

- You may feel hot and need to rest even when you don't want to.

- Your body will need water if you become hot because you sweat. If you sweat a lot, you need to sip about a pint every hour.

- You need to rest long enough to cool down or 'chill out'.

- Afterwards, you will feel tired and you may feel unhappy too.

- Too much 'E' can feel horrible.

- Some people who did not know enough about resting and drinking died after taking 'E'.

- There may be other dangers we do not know yet.

- If the police catch you with 'E', you will get into trouble.

ALCOHOL

Alcohol is a depressant drug. This drug is taken by many people. If they are careful, they may not harm themselves. Drinking too much alcohol can make life very unpleasant and dangerous for the taker and for other people they are with. The law says shops and pubs may not sell you alcohol until you are eighteen years old. Some restaurants can serve you alcohol with a meal if you are sixteen years old. No one under the age of sixteen is allowed to drink alcohol.

Why do people drink alcohol?

- It starts by making you feel light-headed and merry.

- You may talk, sing or shout more than normal.

- Parties and dancing can be more fun.

- Alcohol has more effect if you are not used to it.

- It is fun when you are with other people and you don't overdo it.

The risks and bad points

- If you were unhappy to start of with, it can make you feel worse.

- If you drink alcohol, it is harder to keep your balance or speak clearly.

- If you drink and drive, you cannot control a bike or car properly.

- Your body can get used to alcohol so it takes more to make you feel the effects.

- If you drink too much, you can be sick, lose consciousness or even die.

- Alcohol is not good for your brain, your liver, or your heart.

- Alcohol can be quite expensive.

NICOTINE

The drug in cigarettes and cigars is called nicotine which is a stimulant.
This drug is smoked by many people. Even if smokers do not smoke a lot, they may have problems. You are not allowed to smoke in many places such as trains, libraries and restaurants, although the law does not stop you. You will certainly not be allowed to smoke at school! Most problems from smoking are because it can affect your health.

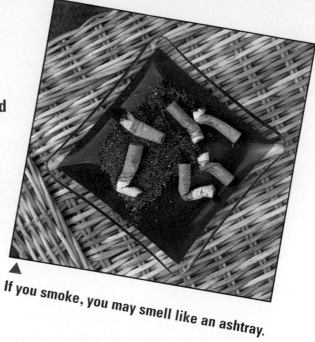

▲
If you smoke, you may smell like an ashtray.

These problems do not always start straight away. You may be older before you become unwell. A lot of people die from the diseases smoking can cause. Some people do not have serious health problems, even if they smoke for many years. But smoking kills more people than any other drug.

Why do people smoke?

- Some people think it looks cool or grown-up to smoke.

- Some people like the taste of smoke.

- It can make you feel light-headed and less anxious.

- People think it's fun to smoke if their friends do too.

- Advertisers make their products look very exciting.

- Smoking makes some people feel more confident.

The risks and bad points

- Your lungs can be damaged by the tar in smoke.

- Breathing someone else's smoke is called passive smoking. You can become ill if you inhale a lot.

- The advertisers make a lot of money from making smoking look good.

- Smoking is expensive.

- It is often very hard to give up.

- Smoking can make you smell horrible.

- It can dull your sense of taste, so food doesn't seem so nice.

- It can cause lung cancer and heart disease.

NICOTINE

AMPHETAMINE

Amphetamine is a stimulant. Some people have amphetamine tablets prescribed by their doctor as a medicine. Amphetamine tablets are sometimes prescribed by doctors as slimming tablets. It is against the law to have it, to buy it, or to sell it if your doctor has not prescribed it for you. Amphetamine powder is often called speed.

▲ Amphetamine powder. If you are not prescribed it by a doctor, it is illegal.

Why do people take amphetamine?

- Amphetamine makes you feel wide awake.

- It makes life seem to go faster.

- You may feel like you have a lot of energy.

- You may feel more confident and cheerful.

- You may be able to concentrate more.

- You may feel you are able to do many things better.

The risks

- You may not feel hungry even when your body needs food.

- Your heartbeat will speed up.

- You may feel anxious, moody and restless.

- If you take a bigger amount, you may feel frightened and want to run away.

- The effects can last for over three hours or more.

- Afterwards, you may feel very tired and depressed.

- If you are found out, you could be in trouble.

AMPHETAMINE

SOLVENTS

Solvent is the name for the strong-smelling chemical that makes glue runny before it dries. Some people sniff all sorts of other chemicals such as lighter fuel, hair spray and nail-varnish remover. Most of these drugs have a very strong smell. All solvents are depressants. Sniffing solvents is very dangerous and lots of people have died doing it. They probably did not know just how dangerous it is. Perhaps nobody had told them.

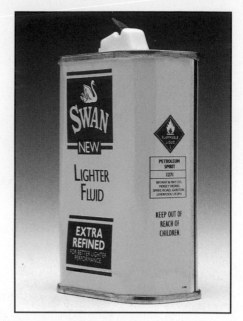

▲ Lighter fuel.

Why do people sniff solvents?

● The effects of solvent sniffing make you feel like you're drunk.

● You may want to 'fool about'.

● The world can seem unreal.

● If a group of people are sniffing, they may want to shout a lot and do things they would not usually do.

The risks and bad points

- Solvents and gases are sometimes sniffed from large plastic bags. This can cause suffocation.

- You can lose your balance or become unconscious and fall.

- Aerosols sprayed into your mouth can freeze your airway and stop you breathing.

- A lot of exercise, such as running or riding a bike, after sniffing solvents can stop your heart from beating.

- You can be sick after sniffing solvents and this can make you choke.

- All of these things have killed sniffers.

- The effects last less than an hour, sometimes only a few minutes.

CANNABIS

Cannabis is a hallucinogen. It is not as difficult to find as some other illegal drugs. Many people have tried this drug. It is against the law to have it, buy it or sell it. The name comes from the cannabis plant. Its dried leaves can be smoked by themselves or with tobacco. Cannabis resin, a solid, hard black or brown block, is a stronger form of the drug. A cannabis cigarette (sometimes called 'joint' or 'spliff') could cost around £1.

▲ The leaves of a cannabis plant can be dried and smoked.

Why do people take cannabis?

● If it is smoked, the effects start very quickly and last up to an hour.

● You feel relaxed and talk a lot.

● Many people who take cannabis enjoy the way it makes them feel.

The risks

- You may forget things.

- It is hard to keep track of time.

- People who are not used to it often feel anxious.

- It is hard to concentrate, and dangerous to drive or ride a bike.

- The effect is not always fun.

- Some people say your health can suffer. The smoke is not good for your lungs.

- It is an illegal drug.

CANNABIS

LSD

LSD is a very strong hallucinogen. LSD can be soaked into small paper squares or can be in the form of a small pill called a microdot. Only a tiny amount has a big effect, called a 'trip'. Once the effect has started, it cannot be stopped and it lasts for many hours. Sometimes, it is enjoyable, but not always. If the trip is unpleasant, it can be very frightening.

▲ This picture shows how small a LSD microdot is.

Why do people take LSD?

- Colours, sounds and tastes all change and seem very strange.

- People who take LSD see the world in a very different way from how they usually see it.

The risks and bad points

- LSD is very strong.

- Sometimes, the effects can come back weeks or even months later. This is called a flashback and it may be very unpleasant.

- It can be harder to stay safe while on a trip because you may not see things as they really are.

- Some people who take LSD see things that are not really there.

- LSD is an illegal drug and you could be in a lot of trouble if caught with it.

MAGIC MUSHROOMS

'Magic mushrooms' is the name for Fly Agaric and Liberty Cap mushrooms. They have chemicals in them that are hallucinogens. The law does not stop people picking and eating magic mushrooms. But if you crush, dry or cook them, they become illegal, and as serious as LSD, heroin, cocaine and Ecstasy.

▲ Liberty cap mushrooms. If you crush, dry or cook these, you are breaking the law.

Why do people take magic mushrooms?

- Magic mushrooms are found easily in the wild.

- The effects when you eat them are a bit like LSD but not so strong.

- The effects start sooner and don't last so long.

- People who pick them don't have to pay for them.

- They make you feel happy.

The risks and bad points

- There are some very poisonous mushrooms that look similar. You might pick these by mistake.

- Stomach pains and being sick are common effects.

- If you are caught with 'prepared' mushrooms, it is a serious crime.

HEROIN

Heroin is a strong painkiller that comes from the sap of the opium poppy. It does not grow in this country. It helps people who are in a lot of pain. Heroin is addictive.

▲ Heroin can be used by doctors to treat pain but is against the law for anyone else to use it.

Why do people take heroin?

- Heroin is a powerful painkiller.

- It makes you feel warm and drowsy.

- Heroin makes you feel happy and stops you worrying for a short time.

- It doesn't make you feel drunk or lose your balance.

The risks

- You can become addicted and then it is really hard to stop.

- If you are caught, you can be in a lot of trouble with the police.

- An overdose can kill you.

- Heroin takers often inject the drug and this can cause problems to their health, such as AIDS and Hepatitis B, if dirty needles are used.

- Stopping taking heroin causes bad withdrawal symptoms.

COCAINE

Cocaine is a strong stimulant. It is usually a white powder that can be dissolved in water and then injected. Another kind of cocaine, called crack, comes in small lumps, sometimes called 'rocks'. Both the powder and the rocks are very expensive and illegal. The law says cocaine is very serious, like heroin, LSD and Ecstasy, so getting caught means big trouble.

▲ Cocaine is usually a white powder.

Why do people take cocaine?

- The effects can last about half an hour.

- It makes you feel wide awake and may make you feel happy.

- You don't feel hungry.

▲ Cocaine is made from the leaves of the coca plant.

The risks

- It may make you panic.

- If cocaine is injected, it can cause serious problems such as AIDS or Hepatitus B if dirty needles are used.

- Afterwards, it makes you feel tired, hungry and unhappy.

- If it is sniffed, it can damage the lining of your nose.

- Taking a lot of cocaine can make you feel frightened.

VIEWPOINTS
RISKS AND DANGERS

The 'fun' factor

Taking a drug when you are not ill and do not need medicine can seem like great fun. Sometimes, it feels exciting because the drug is not allowed. Sometimes, it is because you are with other people and you all want to have a good time. Often, the effects of the drug are fun, or strange. You may get to like them or even find you cannot stop taking the drug.

Knowing the dangers

Sometimes there are risks if you take drugs. This means there may be real danger. You may know about the danger. Or maybe no one has told you. But the danger may be there just the same. Just knowing about a danger does not make it go away. Not all drug taking is dangerous but you need to know the difference between what may be safe and what is not. You need to know what the dangers are. You might want to know how to avoid some of these dangers too. This book has already told you about some of them. If you want to know more, never be afraid to ask your teacher or someone else you trust. Not knowing about a danger can make it worse, a bit like finding your brakes don't work when you are speeding down a hill.

▲ Smoking may not feel harmful, but it is!

Most dangers from drugs are

- taking too much
- not knowing what you are taking
- nasty or harmful effects
- mixing any drug with alcohol, or any other drug
- not being careful about what you are doing
- getting caught
- owing money

Taking too much

If you don't know how much to take, you might take too much by mistake. It is possible to take more than you are used to if the drug is stronger than usual.

With some drugs, when a person has got used to taking them, his or her body can learn to accept a bigger dose. If a person stops taking that drug, his or her body forgets how to cope with a big dose and thinks it is an overdose. An overdose of some drugs, such as sleeping tablets, alcohol or heroin, can kill you.

There are people who are so unhappy they take an overdose because they want to try and kill themselves. Some people have

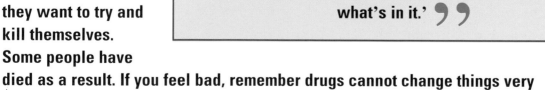

Tom: 'My friends asked me if I wanted to take some speed. I said I wouldn't take take it because I was afraid of what it would do to me. I don't know what's in it.'

died as a result. If you feel bad, remember drugs cannot change things very much. After the effects have worn off, life will be just the same. It is much better to talk to someone when you need help. That way, things can change.

Nasty or harmful effects

Sometimes, the nasty effects of a drug can spoil any fun the drug may give. It is not pleasant to be sick or to have a hangover after drinking too much. People who drink alcohol quite a lot can damage their liver so much that it cannot heal. To drink that much alcohol is a big health risk.

▲ This drug addict may not know how helpful it can be to talk.

Not being careful what you are doing

If you take a drug how can you be sure you will stay safe? You may not know what it is, how strong it is, the effect it may have, what to do to get a nice effect, or how to lessen the risk. It is always important to be careful, whatever you are doing, even if it is only crossing the road or climbing a tree. If you don't take care, you won't be looking after yourself. And that matters. But you can only be careful if you know what's what. So find out!

Injecting drugs

Some people inject themselves with drugs that are not medicines. Injecting is the most dangerous way to take a drug. Mostly it is only doctors and nurses who know how to inject medicines properly. If it is done carelessly, or by someone who does not know how to do it, it can be a huge health risk. It can even kill the person. It is very easy to inject dirt and germs that are too small to see, but are still very harmful.

Getting caught

Getting caught doing something naughty, dangerous or illegal is not fun. Your parents may get angry or punish you. If the police catch you, you could end up going to court if you have done something illegal. That can mean you or your parents are fined, and they will have to pay money to the court. For people who are seventeen years old or more, it may even mean going to some kind of prison. You risk prison if caught with Ecstasy, heroin, cocaine, crack or LSD. Cannabis is also illegal and, if you have a lot and give some to your friends, you can also be in serious trouble. How you are punished depends on how much of the drug you are caught with, whether you have been caught with it before and if the police think you were going to sell it to somebody else.

▲ If caught at school, you may even get expelled.

Criminal record

If the court finds you are guilty of breaking the law, they keep a record of it. This can stop you getting some kinds of jobs, or going to some countries such as the USA. The record they keep is called your 'criminal record'. You cannot get rid of a criminal record, so it is worth making sure you do not get one.

> 66 Sammy: 'My parents caught me with some cannabis in my room. They were very angry with me and I felt really bad. They threatened to go to the police if I carried on taking it.' 99

DRUG LAWS

This page explains some of the laws that say which drugs are allowed and which are not.

Medicines

You can buy many medicines at the chemist, but there are some which you are not allowed to have unless the doctor says so. These are called restricted drugs. There will be instructions and your name on the packet or bottle. You may have to pay for them. There are some drugs which the law only allows doctors to handle. These are usually powerful medicines. Heroin is one of these.

Legal drugs

The most common legal drugs that are not medicines, are caffeine, alcohol and nicotine. Solvents, poppers and GHB are also legal to have, although how you get hold of them is another thing. The law does not allow you to buy alcohol from a pub or shop until you are eighteen. Before that, you are allowed to try it, but not in a pub and you must not buy it yourself. The only alcohol you can buy before you are eighteen is beer, cider or perry to drink with a meal in a restaurant.

▲ If the doctor thinks you need a restricted drug, he or she will give you a prescription.

Solvents

Shops are not allowed to sell solvents to anyone under the age of eighteen if the shopkeeper thinks they are going to be sniffed.

Nicotine

is an addictive drug. Shops are only allowed to sell it to people who are over 16, even if it is for someone else.

Poppers are legal but, as with all ▲ drugs, you take a risk if you take them.

Class A (the most serious)	Class B (the middle group)	Class C (not as serious)
heroin, methadone, opium, cocaine, crack, LSD, Ecstasy, prepared magic mushrooms, any class B drug that is injected	amphetamine (speed), cannabis (resin, grass and oil), barbiturates (sleeping tablets), codeine	mild amphetamine, tranquillizers, anabolic steroids
Maximum penalties Possession: **7 years in prison + fine** Trafficking: **life + fine**	**Maximum penalties** Possession: **5 years in prison + fine** Trafficking: **14 years in prison + fine**	**Maximum penalties** Possession: **2 years in prison + fine** Trafficking: **5 years in prison + fine**

The law that restricts these drugs is called the Misuse of Drugs Act, 1971.

Illegal drugs

These drugs are against the law unless your doctor gives you a prescription for them. Many of the drugs in this table are not allowed, even for doctors. No one is allowed to have cocaine, crack, LSD, Ecstasy, cannabis or magic mushrooms that are crushed or dried. They are not medicines.

▲ LSD, or 'trips' in paper squares.

WHAT PEOPLE THINK ABOUT DRUGS

What people may think when they don't know much about drugs...

When people feel strongly about a subject, they sometimes think they know what is right and what is wrong. They may not know much about drugs, but they still think they are bad. They may not think of alcohol or paracetamol as drugs. When they hear of drug problems, they may not think of the accidents and illnesses that occur due to using legal drugs. They think of young people trying illegal drugs and they think it should be stopped. They may feel frightened of the effects illegal drugs can have. They may think young people should be told to say 'No' to drugs. If people know about drugs, it might help them keep calm when they talk about it. Perhaps you can tell adults you know about this book and what you have learned.

... and what they may think when they know a lot about drugs

People who know a lot about drugs are often not as worried. They know drugs can be dangerous. They know medicines and legal drugs can be risky. But when you know about something, it is not as frightening. Adults are not always sensible – some smoke, some drink and then drive, and some may even take illegal drugs. People who know about drugs may feel young people need to know the facts.

It's good to talk about drugs with your parents or other adults and listen to their opinions.

▼

Different opinions

Not everyone agrees about what drugs should be used and how. For example, in this country, alcohol is a legal drug. In Islamic countries, such as Iran, and Iraq, alcohol is illegal. Mormons try not to have any drugs at all, not even the caffeine in coffee or cola drinks. Some people would like more drugs to be made illegal. Others would like drugs such as cannabis to be legalized. Newspapers, politicians, parents and teachers have all discussed drugs and often they can't agree. Just as some people smoke and others choose not to, some people choose to try illegal drugs, while others would not go near them.

Being honest

Many people think the best thing is to be honest about drugs. If you know the truth, you can make your own choice. If you know the risks, and you want to be sure to stay safe, you can choose not to take a drug. It is the only way to be certain you will come to no harm. If you take a risk, at least you will know what you are doing. Drugs are not always bad news.

◀ In The Netherlands, cannabis is a legal drug. This man has won many prizes for his plants.

THE GOOD AND BAD NEWS

The good news about drugs

If you are ill and you are careful about which medicine you take, and make sure the dose is right, it can make you well. It may even save your life if the illness is a very serious one. If you are at a wedding or drinking wine with a meal, alcohol need not cause any problems. A lot of people drink in a sensible way. Some people try illegal drugs. The risks are real, but they are careful and enjoy what they do. If they don't have any problems, they are either careful or just lucky. But even being careful does not make all the risks go away.

Not such good news

Sometimes, drugs are used for bad reasons. They can't make up for lost sleep, or not having good food or exercise. You need to take care of your health and a drug can't do that for you (unless it's proper medicine). If you just take a drug because you feel fed up or miserable, it won't help for long and it may stop you thinking about what you can do to put things right or make them better. Talking about a problem is far more helpful than trying to forget it by using drugs.

If people take a drug for a bad reason, or without thinking, or without reading the instructions on the medicine bottle, they are taking a risk.

The bad news about drugs

Lots of things can go wrong. The effect may not be what you thought it would be, the drug might not be what the person said it was and you may not have enough money to pay for it. The person who sells you a drug does not care about your health or safety as long as you pay! If you take a depressant drug, you may lose your balance and not be able to cross the road safely.

A certain way to stay safe from harm or danger is not to take drugs at all. Otherwise there is always some risk. It is a fact that many people take drugs, but this doesn't mean that it's any less dangerous.

Deaths

Some people who have tried illegal drugs have died. Most of these deaths are connected with the use of heroin or Ecstasy. Solvents have killed many more people who probably did not realize the risks. Alcohol and nicotine kill more people than all other drugs put together.

This boy is sniffing glue and ▶ endangering his health.

KEEPING SAFE

Piggy in the Middle that's you!

Sometimes, it is hard to make a choice. All your friends may be doing something and you want to do it too. Perhaps you worry about what other people will think of you so you don't weigh up the benefits and risks properly. Maybe you just want to know what a drug is like so you try it. Perhaps one day you feel bad and want a 'lift'. You are human after all! But don't forget you are important and nobody in the world can look after you as well as you can.

Here is a list of things you may want to think about.

- You can have fun in many safe ways. Think of what you enjoy doing.
- By knowing how to take care, you will be less at risk from harming yourself.
- Medicines can help you feel better, but it's best to ask for advice from your doctor.
- Ask for help or a chat when you feel bad or worried.
- Remember how important your health is.
- Remember how important you are!
- Never be afraid to ask an adult for help and advice.
- Only do what you want to, not what someone tries to make you do.

▲ Choose friends who care about you.

Keeping safe is what matters

The really important thing is for you to keep healthy and stay safe. There are many risks and dangers in the world and drugs are just a part of that. If you know the facts, and you are really careful, then drugs need not be something to be frightened of or to worry about. Whether the drug is prescribed by a doctor, a legal drug or an illegal one, it cannot hurt you if you don't take it. If you do take it, then you need to weigh the risks carefully or you may be in danger. You are unique and worth looking after! Take good care of yourself, whatever you are doing.

How do you say what you want to say?

Tell people how you feel. Say what you want. Don't be pushed or walked on by others. Look at this girl saying what she wants to, gently and firmly. You can disagree with someone without making enemies! Even if you talk like this, you may not always get what you want.

NOTES FOR TEACHERS

The Department for Education and Employment (DfEE) have informed schools that all young people need accurate information upon which to base their decisions about drug use, and that teaching about drugs is generally best provided as part of an integrated programme of health education for children of all ages. They have stated that the purpose of drug education should be to give young people the knowledge, skills and attitudes to appreciate the benefits of a healthy lifestyle and relate these to their own actions, both now and in the future.

This book attempts to provide some accurate information about drugs which may be appropriate to the needs of teenage pupils. It may make a contribution to the drugs education of the reader, although it is not intended to give the impression of being a comprehensive or complete programme. It is not expected that any person will read this book from cover to cover. However, it may be beneficial to dip into factual information and the ideas it contains. The tone of the book has been carefully developed and is not intended to judge or restrict; the approach avoids trying to impose 'correct' or healthy behaviour upon the readers. The focus is upon the value of each individual person as well as upon drugs that may be encountered. The central aim is to build readers' confidence in their own capacity for rational, careful and informed decisions.

However, two ingredients of drug education which are vital but not included here are opportunities for discussion, and for skills acquisition and practice. In order to fulfil the purpose of drug education as specified by the DfEE, it will be necessary for teachers to provide a planned programme, addressing knowledge and skills, as well as providing opportunities to consider a range of attitudes to drugs. Teachers are encouraged to read the DfEE documents listed on page 46 and to consider how the contents of this book may form a part of the drugs education programme.

From time to time, facts and ideas are touched upon only fleetingly, and in some cases these may usefully be expanded upon in discussion either with individual, group or whole class.

For example

● You may wish to explore in greater depth the use of tranquillizers (benzodiazepines), or to consider other forms of medication familiar to pupils, such as Ventolin used commonly by asthma sufferers and Insulin used by diabetics. It is worth considering both their value and what could go wrong.

● It may help to expand upon how legal drugs are purchased or otherwise obtained. Tobacco sales are restricted to over sixteens. It is the seller, not the buyer, who commits an offence. With alcohol, both buyer and seller would be in the wrong if the buyer were under age. If a person were to steal a 'legal' drug, that drug would then be an illegal possession.

● GHB is briefly mentioned. This is a liquid with the unwieldy name of gammahydroxybutyrate. It is classed as a medicine and therefore controlled under the Medicines Act. Amylnitrite, one of the drugs known as 'poppers' is also restricted under the Medicines Act. This means that unauthorized production of both is an offence, as is supply of either outside of pharmacy. Butylnitrite is not so restricted.

● The Intoxicating Substances Supply Act 1985 forbids sale of solvents to people under eighteen if the seller 'knows or suspects' that the buyer is going to use them for intoxicating purposes.

GLOSSARY

Alcohol
Alcohol is the drug in drinks, such as beer, wine and spirits which people over eighteen are allowed to buy in pubs. Alcohol can make you drunk.

Anabolic Steroids
A group of strong hormone drugs that doctors can prescribe. Sometimes, athletes take them because they believe the drugs will make their muscles stronger.

Caffeine
A stimulant drug in tea, coffee, some soft drinks and some medicines. It makes you feel less sleepy and makes your heart beat faster.

Chill out
This means resting when you are too hot to cool down. Sometimes, at dances there is a special room or area for chilling out.

Depressant
A depressant drug slows down the messages you send along your nervous system. It may make you sleepy too.

Dose
The amount of a drug taken at one time. A bigger dose usually has a bigger effect. If it is too much, it is called an overdose. Doctors know what dose is safe.

Drug trafficking
An illegal business that buys and sells drugs.

GHB
A short name for Gammahydroxybutyrate. GHB is a legal, liquid anaesthetic which can send you to sleep. It can also make you sick and is more dangerous if you also drink alcohol. It is hard to be sure of the dose.

Hangover
A hangover is the horrible feeling you get hours after you have had a lot of alcohol to drink. It can be a headache, a tummy ache, feeling sick and feeling dizzy.

Injected
This means using a needle and a syringe to push the drug into the body. Only liquids can be injected.

Liver
A special part of the body, called an organ. Your liver helps use the food you eat to keep you well and cleans the blood from some poisons. You only have one liver, so your body can't do without it.

Nervous system
A network of nerves inside you for sending messages between your body and your brain.

Nicotine
A very strong, addictive, stimulant drug in tobacco.

Painkillers
Drugs that stop pain or lessen it. They don't heal the body, though!

Poppers
'Poppers' is the nickname for amyl and butyl nitrite – sweet-smelling, legal, liquid drugs some people buy to sniff. The effect lasts 2–5 minutes and makes you feel dizzy and light-headed.

Prescription
A form that your doctor gives to you so that you can get a certain drug from a chemist.

Resin
A solid substance that has been taken straight from the plant.

Stimulant
A stimulant drug speeds up the messages you send along your nervous system. It makes it hard to sleep.

Suffocation
Suffocation is the name for dying when someone doesn't have enough oxygen to breathe.

Syringe
This is a small, plastic tube with a needle on the end which doctors and nurses use to inject medicines into patients.

Tar
This is thick, black, sticky stuff. Tiny droplets of tar are in cigarette smoke. This can clog a smoker's lungs and stop them working properly. The amount of tar in the cigarettes is sometimes printed on the packet.

Trip
The name for the experience you have on LSD. A trip can last 12 hours and can be a 'good trip' or a 'bad trip'. Bad trips can be very frightening. 'Good trip' does not mean safe.

Unconscious
When you are unaware of what is going on around you.

Withdrawal symptoms
The bad feelings people get when they stop taking an addictive drug.

FURTHER INFORMATION

Books to Read

For young readers
Hot Topics: Drugs by Terry Brown and Adrian King (Aladdin, 1995)
We're Talking About Alcohol by Jenny Bryan (Wayland, 1995)
We're Talking About Drugs by Jenny Bryan (Wayland, 1995)
We're Talking About Smoking by Karen Byrant-Mole (Wayland, 1995)
What Do You Know About Drugs by Pete Saunders and Steve Myers (Watts, 1995)

For adults
The following three documents were published by the Department for Education and Employment in May 1995 and are available to schools at no charge from the DfEE Publications Unit, Tel: 0171 510 0150
Circular 4/95: Drug Prevention and Schools
Drug Education: Curriculum Guidance for Schools
Digest of Drugs Education Resources for Schools

Curriculum Guidance 5: Health Education (The National Curriculum Council, 1990)
Drug Abuse Briefing (ISDD, teacher's edition, 1996)
Drugs Issues for Schools by Colin Chapman (ISDD, 2nd edition)
Special Health by Combes and Craft (The Health Education Authority) A source book for teachers of pupils with learning difficulties
Special Needs and Drug Education by Richard Ives. Teacher's pack. Available direct from the publisher. Tel: 0171 263 0510
Street Drugs by Andrew Tyler (New English Library)

National Agencies

National Drugs Helpline Tel: 0800 776600

Institute For The Study of Drug Dependence (ISDD)
Waterbridge House, 32-36 Loman Street, London, SE1 0EE.
Tel: 0171 928 1211

Drug Education Practitioners Forum, Drugs Education and Training Service,
Drug and Alcohol Services, Chadwell Heath Hospital,
Grove Road, Chadwell Heath, Romford, RM6 4XH.
Tel: 0181 597 2802

Other useful information
The Drugs Information Poster (Educational Television Co., 1995)
Drug Data (interactive PC or Amiga computer programme) (Healthwise, 1994)

INDEX